DETECTIVE'S TOOLS

ANDERS HANSON

Consulting Editor, Diane Craig, M.A./Reading Specialist

A Division of ABDO
ABDO
Publishing Company

visit us at www.abdopublishing.com

Published by ABDO Publishing Company, a division of ABDO,
P.O. Box 398166, Minneapolis, Minnesota 55439. Copyright © 2014
by Abdo Consulting Group, Inc. International copyrights reserved in all
countries. No part of this book may be reproduced in any form without
written permission from the publisher. Super SandCastle™
is a trademark and logo of ABDO Publishing Company.

Printed in the United States of America,
North Mankato, Minnesota
102013
012014

♺ PRINTED ON RECYCLED PAPER

Editor: Liz Salzmann
Content Developer: Nancy Tuminelly
Photo Credits: Shutterstock

Library of Congress Cataloging-in-Publication Data

Hanson, Anders.
 Detective's tools / Anders Hanson.
   pages cm. -- (More professional tools)
 Audience: Ages 5-10.
 ISBN 978-1-62403-071-0
1. Criminal investigation--Juvenile literature. 2. Detectives--Juvenile literature. 3. Police--Equipment and supplies--Juvenile literature. I. Title.
 HV8073.8.H364 2014
 363.25028'4--dc23
                2013022537

Super SandCastle™ books are created by a team of professional
educators, reading specialists, and content developers around five
essential components—phonemic awareness, phonics, vocabulary,
text comprehension, and fluency—to assist young readers as they
develop reading skills and strategies and increase their general
knowledge. All books are written, reviewed, and leveled for guided
reading, early reading intervention, and Accelerated Reader®
programs for use in shared, guided, and independent reading and
writing activities to support a balanced approach to literacy
instruction.

CONTENTS

MEET A DETECTIVE!

WHAT DOES A DETECTIVE DO?

Detectives solve crimes.

When a crime is committed, detectives make a list of **suspects**. Then they try to find **evidence** that connects a suspect to the crime. If they find enough evidence, they arrest the suspect.

WHY DO DETECTIVES NEED TOOLS?

Tools help detectives find, collect, and store evidence.

DETECTIVE'S TOOLS

Camera

Fingerprint Kit

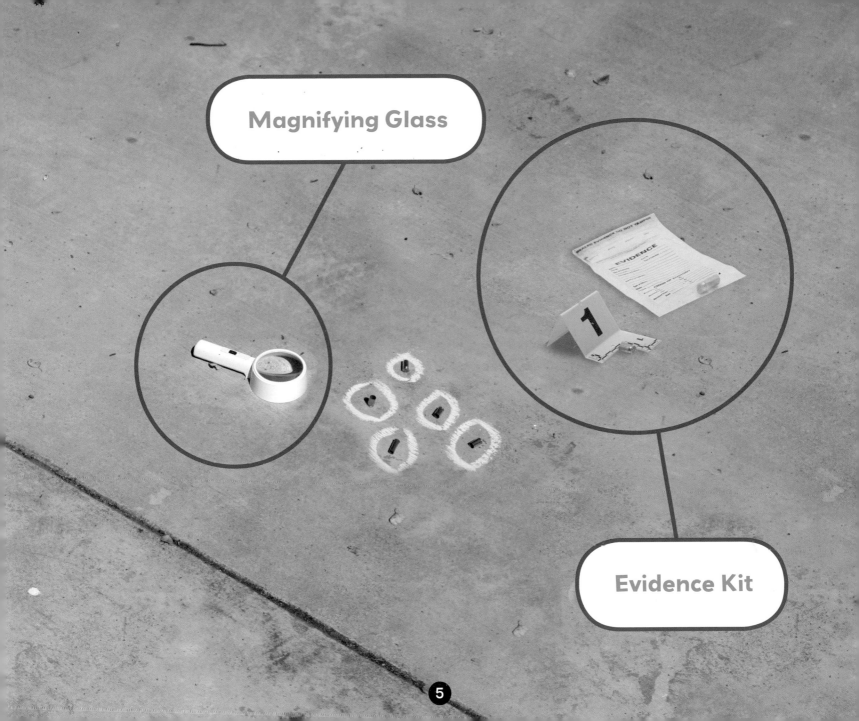

Magnifying Glass

Evidence Kit

FINGERPRINT KIT

brush

fingerprint

powder

Fingerprint kits reveal hidden fingerprints.

Every fingertip has a pattern of **ridges** on it. When we touch something, the ridges leave a mark. That is a fingerprint.

Fingerprints are light and hard to see. Detectives find fingerprints by lightly brushing them with dark powder. The powder sticks to the prints. That makes the fingerprints dark.

Jenna is dusting for fingerprints. If she finds any, she'll scan them into a computer.

Sara tries to match a mystery print to a known print. If she finds a match, she'll know whose finger left the print!

MAGNIFYING GLASS

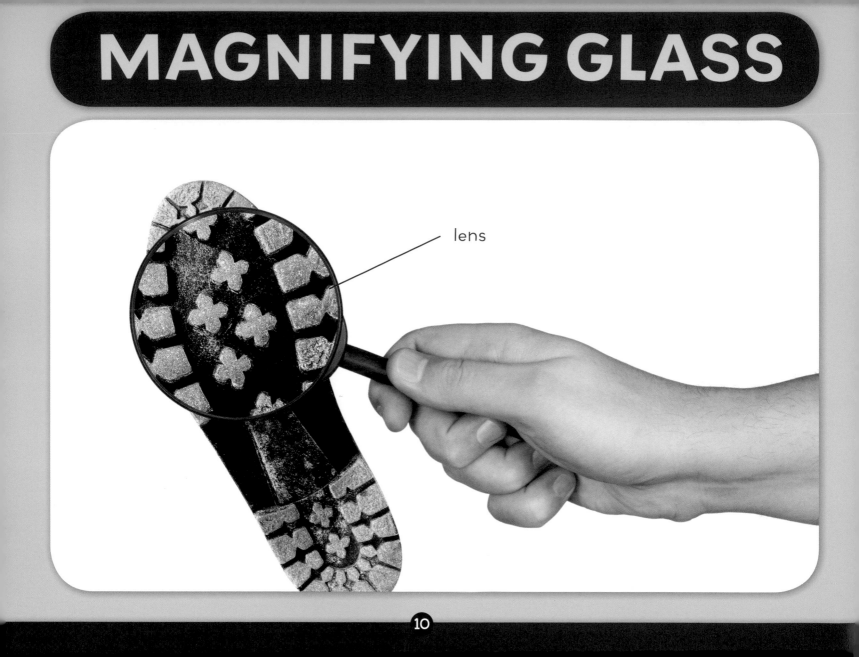

lens

Magnifying glasses make things look bigger.

Hidden clues could be anywhere. They are often very small. Eyes alone aren't always able to spot them.

Detectives use magnifying glasses to get a better look at things.

Traci looks at a fingerprint on a sheet of paper.
She uses a magnifying glass to get a better look.

Jessica checks some money. She thinks it may be fake. She gets a closer look with a magnifying glass.

EVIDENCE KIT

photo marker

evidence bag

scale

Detectives use evidence kits to organize and store evidence.

Evidence kits have many tools that help detectives. **Photo** markers label evidence found at the scene. Scales measure the size of the evidence. Evidence is **photographed** after being marked and measured. Then it is sealed in evidence bags.

Amanda is at a crime scene. She circles important objects. Then she places a photo marker next to each one.

Katy is organizing evidence. She labels each object and notes anything unusual about it.

CAMERA

shutter

lens

grip

Detectives use cameras to record evidence.

Detectives take a lot of **photos**. They may record a **suspect's** activities. Or they may take pictures of a crime scene.

Photos are an important type of **evidence**.

Cari takes pictures of a **suspect**. She uses a **telephoto lens** so the suspect won't see her taking the pictures.

Craig is a detective. He investigates a crime scene.
Jack takes pictures of the scene with a camera.

MATCH THE WORDS TO THE PICTURES!

The answers are on the bottom of the page.

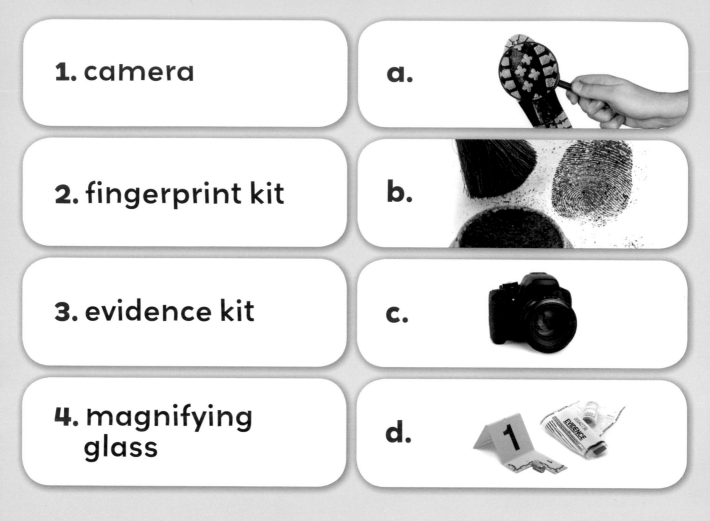

1. camera

a.

2. fingerprint kit

b.

3. evidence kit

c.

4. magnifying glass

d.

Answers: 1) c 2) b 3) d 4) a

TEST YOUR TOOL KNOWLEDGE!

The answers are on the bottom of the page.

1.

People have **ridges** on their fingertips.

TRUE OR FALSE?

2.

Magnifying glasses make things look smaller.

TRUE OR FALSE?

3.

Photo markers label **evidence**.

TRUE OR FALSE?

4.

Cameras record evidence.

TRUE OR FALSE?

TOOL QUIZ

Answers: 1) true   2) false   3) true   4) true

GLOSSARY

evidence – facts and information that prove whether something is true.

investigate – to search for and study clues and evidence to learn the facts about a crime.

loop – something shaped like a circle made by a rope, string, or thread.

photo – a picture made using a camera.

photograph – to make a picture using a camera.

ridge – a narrow, raised area on the surface of something.

scan – to enter a picture or image into a computer.

suspect – a person who is thought to have committed a crime.

telephoto lens – a camera lens that makes pictures of distant objects so they look like they are much closer.

unique – not the same as anything else.

whorl – something that whirls or winds around a center.